THE TEN BAMBOO STUDIO
A Chinese Masterpiece

THE PRINTS OF
THE TEN BAMBOO STUDIO

followed by Plates from the
KAEMPFER SERIES
and
PERFECT HARMONY

Presentation
and Commentary by
Joseph Vedlich

OMEGA BOOKS

This edition published 1984 by Omega Books Ltd,
1 West Street, Ware, Hertfordshire,
under licence from the proprietor,
Productions Liber SA, Fribourg.

ISBN 1-85007-060-1

Printed in Italy

Translation by Peter J. Tallon.

We wish to thank M. and Mme. Beurdeley and M. Jean Fribourg for the valuable advice which they have kindly given us.

Readers seeking fuller information should consult their works, in particular Arts de la Chine *(J. Fribourg),* La céramique chinoise *and* L'amateur chinois *(C. and M. Beurdeley), all of which are published by L'Office du Livre, Fribourg.*

The captions for plates 1 to 4 of Perfect Harmony *were adapted, with the kind consent of the author and the publisher, from the third of the above-mentioned works.*

J. V.

Plates from the Studio of the Ten Bamboos *and the* Kaempfer Series *by courtesy of the Trustees of the British Museum, London.*

Ektas: British Museum, London.

Plates from Perfect Harmony *reproduced by kind permission of the Keepers of the Department of Chinese Antiquities at the Musée Guimet.*

Ektas: Réunion des Musées Nationaux, Paris.

The narrow road towards understanding of Chinese realities

China—the Middle Empire—is a country that has been and still is closed to the world for more than one reason; at one time because it was so far away, today because of political reasons. Westerners, who have learned their reasoning from Aristotle, have difficulty understanding the country, and often wrongly judge the Chinese way of seeing man and the world. A secret key to gain access to Chinese culture is the language—closed also by its outer aspect to the person who is not capable of making the effort of putting aside Western cultural heritage and our concept of the written word. Learning the language is the hardest method of making contact with Chinese culture; approaching it via the arts is infinitely more pleasant.

Chinese arts cover a huge field which dates back to the dawn of time. The first Neolithic pottery was discovered in Northern China a few years ago; it dates from four thousand years BC. Painting began approximately in the second century BC, as frescoes on tombs have proved; the art flourished from the sixth century AD with the "Six Principles" on painting, written by the painter Ksi He. Painting became the art of minute detail and perfection, and was a discipline reserved for the elite of the country, protected by the emperors. It was an integral part of the intellectual training of civil servants, along with poetry, calligraphy and music. Woodcuts developed in parallel to painting, although at the beginning they were linked partly to other expressions.

There are no Chinese prints dating from before the ninth century AD still extant. However, several matrices and engraved stones give us an exact idea of the technique and the quality of the oldest prints. From the ninth century AD onwards, the process was used for printing books. The discovery of paper and ink, and the use of wooden plates instead of stone, gave a tremendous impetus to printing. Later, the techniques were perfected, and the trade of engraver developed separately from that of painter. By the 16th century, complete series of prints were in circulation, coming off the presses by the thousand.

Techniques reached their peak in the 17th century. Only one block was used with the different colours spread over; engravers continued to use several successive plates. Perfection in printing reached such a degree that it became difficult to distinguish between a woodcut and an original water colour. The best example is provided by the *Studio of the Ten Bamboos* album.

The Studio of the Ten Bamboos album of woodcuts

This album was engraved on wooden plates by the master engraver Hou Yue-ts'ong, a scholar of many talents, who, after having retired from government service, set up shop in Nanking. He gathered around him several painter friends and together they composed an album of the works of famous artists. The Studio of the Ten Bamboos was the house where the little group met. The publisher's intention was probably to print a manual for use by debutant painters, to familiarize them with the techniques of the old masters. Different dates on certain prints give the clue to this magnificent work's printing as the beginning of the 17th century, probably 1619.

The Album includes eight parts printed in one, two or three colours, each made up of twenty prints, classified according to the subject: fruits, birds, orchids, bamboos, plum-tree flowers, stones. Most of the subjects were painted for the album and the hand of several artists can be recognized. Each print is accompanied by a poem or text which is related to the illustration and which is printed on a separate page. The entire album includes more than 180 illustrations and the same number of pages of text.

A first complete edition of the work appeared in 1643, with a preface dated 1633. Unfortunately, there is no longer a complete copy available. It was printed with the original plates, but was the only one, later editions being reprinted with certain newly-engraved plates. At the beginning of the 17th century, Nanking was ravaged by the Manchu invasion. Hou Yue-ts'ong's workshop was burnt, as well as many of the plates from the Studio of the Ten Bamboos album. The master's nephew re-engraved the missing plates and the album was reprinted several times, even clandestinely. In 1715, it was presented with a new preface replacing that of 1633. In it, the publisher complained bitterly:

"Every book leaving this house is a marvel of calligraphy and the reproductions are widely appreciated. We have made a general collection of brush-work paintings. The paintings are poems, and the poems are paintings. They bear the spirit and the reflection of nature. We have spent large sums of money and have not spared our efforts. Recently, an unscrupulous group stole our name, used it in intrigues and tried to make money out of it."

The album was reprinted later in China and Japan, using one or the other preface, in 1817 and 1879, with new woodcuts of poor quality. Examples are held by the British Museum in London, the Bibliothèque Nationale in Paris and some private collectors.

The so-called "Kaempfer" series

Although Chinese, this series of 29 prints of astounding beauty reached Europe via Japan in 1692. At the beginning of the 17th century, the Empire of the Rising Sun was visited by a handful of Europeans—Dutch and Portuguese— merchants and missionaries. But, following domestic troubles, Japan closed itself off to foreigners and after

1639 only Chinese and Dutch were allowed a trading post in Nagasaki. Japan remained closed to all others until 1835! Nevertheless, at the end of the 17th century, a German, Doctor Kaempfer, working for the Dutch fleet, was allowed to disembark in Nagasaki and purchase this magnificent series of prints, which represented greetings cards. The cards were exported in great quantities to Japan by Chinese traders; they could still be found on the Japanese market at the end of the 18th century.

Doctor Kaempfer was probably attracted as much by the aesthetic value of these prints as by their documentary value, which was inappreciable to Western naturalists. When he died, the series was bought by the Sloane family which presented it to the British Museum at its founding. It remained locked in a drawer for two centuries, away from the light, which explains the perfect condition of the colour prints. Shortly after 1900, the Curator of the Far East Department discovered the hidden treasure. Originally, the series probably contained more than 29 pieces, although the Kaempfer series is the most complete we know of.

Some single pieces were bought later by other travellers either in China or Japan. In the 18th century, a Jesuit sent a collection of Chinese prints to a friend in France. Among other things, it included some of the prints from the Kaempfer series. The Jesuit made a significant remark about them, which gives us a good idea of the highly-developed taste of the Chinese: "The third lot of paintings is of the most common type and, in China, was sold to the lower classes and inhabitants of the countryside..."

The Chinese were formalists and bound to observe a large number of rules and rites. They used time-honoured formulae to express their wishes and feelings for various events. The publisher of this series of greetings cards was Ting Lean-sien, a famous scholar, writer and draughtsman, calligrapher and engraver. Some plates indicate "written by" or "drawn by", as well as bearing a calligraphic inscription. These prints pre-date those of the Studio of the Ten Bamboos, taking their inspiration from the 17th century. Pirated editions appeared later, without an author's name.

"Perfect harmony"

This is the eloquent title of a series of ten paintings on silk, contained in a charming casket, which came to Europe from China, probably via the East India Company on the Silk Route. This astonishing collection was painted by Yun p'ing, daughter of the famous painter Yun Chow, and dates from 1670.

The father was the uncontested master of floral compositions, which were far more than the simple botanical studies common in the 17th century. He taught the art of the paint brush to his daughter, who soon reached his level of perfection. Tch'an painting is a genuine mystical art which seeks to discover the relationship which exists between nature and man. Each leaf, each flower presents a subtle difference and is the result of profound reflection. The sources of Tch'an painting are Indian and Chinese—Tch'an doctrine teaches that the body of Buddha is present in every aspect of nature, which must be meditated on to reach the great void—the preparatory stage for the union with the supreme truth.

The literary quality of the thoughts which accompany the paintings bears no argument; it is proof of the artist's remarkable knowledge. He was able to observe the world of flowers and insects, and had a thorough knowledge of the teachings of the ancient philosophers. He was able to add a poetic commentary to each image, playing with every symbol which reflects the image of the human being in nature.

It was very rare for a woman to be a painter in ancient China, as painting was an official art, studied by civil servants. Women rarely had the opportunity of receiving complete training in the field. Both Yun p'ing and her sister Yun Chou (who was also a famous poetess) lived in an artistic environment from their earliest youth, and were remarkable artists from the beginning of the Ts'ing period.

This is the first time that plates from the "Perfect Harmony" have been published in a book and we are proud to present them.

Confucianism. The "Secret Key"

The woodcuts and paintings reproduced in this book are accompanied by numerous extracts from the work of Confucius or of different masters of his school. The texts will certainly help the reader to understand the ideas, which, for the non-initiated, appear to have a curious train of thought. It is a fact that the symbolism of Chinese painting springs from Confucianism, and if the two were separated, the symbolism would be lost in useless considerations.

K'ong-tsu—latinized to Confucius by the Jesuit fathers—was born more than two and a half thousand years ago. His prodigious influence on Chinese and Asiatic thinking is still apparent today. Little is known of his life. The essential is contained in his *Conversations* with his disciples, large extracts from which appear here. He lived at the time of the downfall of the Zou empire, which was torn by internal rivalries, corruption, moral decadence and war. His deep thinking helped define the immutable principles of morals and natural law, of which observation and respect could cure the ills of his time.

He insisted on virtue as the answer to moral corruption, defined moral precepts and a large number of factors that were to be the starting point for the development of Confucianism. The aims of his thinking were to distinguish between good and evil, between truth and lie, between vice and virtue, the essential and the accessory, to define justice, good faith, turpitude and natural law. He sought to define the real and true nature of man, in harmony with the order of things established by Heaven; if man conformed, corruption and disorder would disappear to be replaced by harmony and accord. Although having lived two centuries before Aristotle, he managed to define the same concepts using a different method. If Aristotle was the father of logic—the formal analysis of knowledge, mainly the search for the meaning of words—Confucius was a pure empirical moralist, who liked to hold loose discussions with his disciples, constantly changing the subject, himself interrogating those around him. He never replied by an argument, but with an image drawn from experience. If Aristotle is the spiritual father of the West, profoundly inspiring even European Marxists, who claim no influence from him at all, it can be said that Confucius plays the same role in Asia. None of his critics who have sought the impossible—to uproot his way of thinking and of seeing the world—have succeeded in freeing themselves of his heritage; Maoism itself is no more than a surrogate philosophy, derived from Confucianism.

The major part of Confucius' teaching and of his school is contained in the "Four Books"—the "Great Study", the "Constant Middle", the "Conversations of Confucius and his disciples" and the "Works of Meng Tsu", which along with the five "King", form the basis of Chinese classical teaching.   *J. V.*

The Prints of
The Ten Bamboo Studio

Selected texts from

The Great Study

The Constant Middle

*Conversations between
Confucius and his disciples*

TWO MANDARIN BRANCHES

This remarkable composition with five mandarins has not been fully printed, as can be seen from the fruits which are merely sketched in with the same ink as the veins of the leaves. The range of greens used here is also remarkable.

THE GREAT STUDY

The Great Study is the work of Confucius and his disciples. It is like the door which opens the way to virtue. The seeker of wisdom who begins by studying this book is little likely to stray from the right path.

"The way of the Great Study, that is, what man must apply himself from his youth onwards to know and practice, consists of three things, which are: to make shine inside oneself the glittering virtues that nature puts into every soul; to transform other men; and to fix the highest perfection as a goal."

"One must distinguish between the principal thing and the accessory in every way, and in affairs between the beginning and the end. He who knows how to place everything according to its rank, is not far from the way of the Great Study or from perfection. Once the nature of things has been closely examined, knowledge reaches its highest degree. Once knowledge has reached its highest degree, will-power becomes perfect. Once will-power is perfect, the beating of the heart becomes steady, and the whole man is free of fault. After having corrected himself, man establishes order in the family. Once order reigns in the family, the principality is well governed, and soon all the empire lives in harmony. He who neglects the principal thing—his own person—cannot properly regulate the things that depend on it—his family and the principality. Never has a man who cares little for what he should love the most—his family—governed with diligence that which is the least dear to him—his principality or empire."

16

FLOWERY BRANCH

This plate is probably from one of the early editions. It is incomplete, as neither the color of the flower petals nor that of the fruit has been printed.

"If we want to extend our knowledge as far as possible, we must examine things and seek their reason for being. There is no man who is not intelligent enough to acquire knowledge, and there is nothing on earth that does not have its reason for being. But he who has not properly studied the reason of things, will only have an imperfect knowledge of reason. Therefore, from the beginning, the Great Study advises the student to examine everything with which he is in contact and to use the knowledge that he has already to deeper penetrate its reason for being, to continue his search to the furthest limits. When he has done for a long time all that is in his power, and that one fine day he comes to understand everything perfectly, then the interior and exterior of things, everything they possess that is subtle or apparent, all this will become known to him. The innate principles of the soul and their application will no longer be hidden from him. This is called *having penetrated the nature of things.* It is also called *the highest point of knowledge.*"

"When a vicious man is alone he does evil; there is nothing he does not deny himself. If he sees a wise man, he immediately hides his appearance and nastiness, and pretends to be virtuous. But the wise man sees through his intentions, as if he were seeing the bottom of his heart. What is the point of this dissimulation? It is as the proverb says: *The inside always manifests itself on the outside.* Therefore the wise man takes great care to control his most secret thoughts and actions. The riches of a family can be he seen in the ornaments which decorate the house. In the same way, a man's virtue shows in all his person; the swelling of his heart reflects on his body. This is why the disciple of wisdom takes care to make his will perfect."

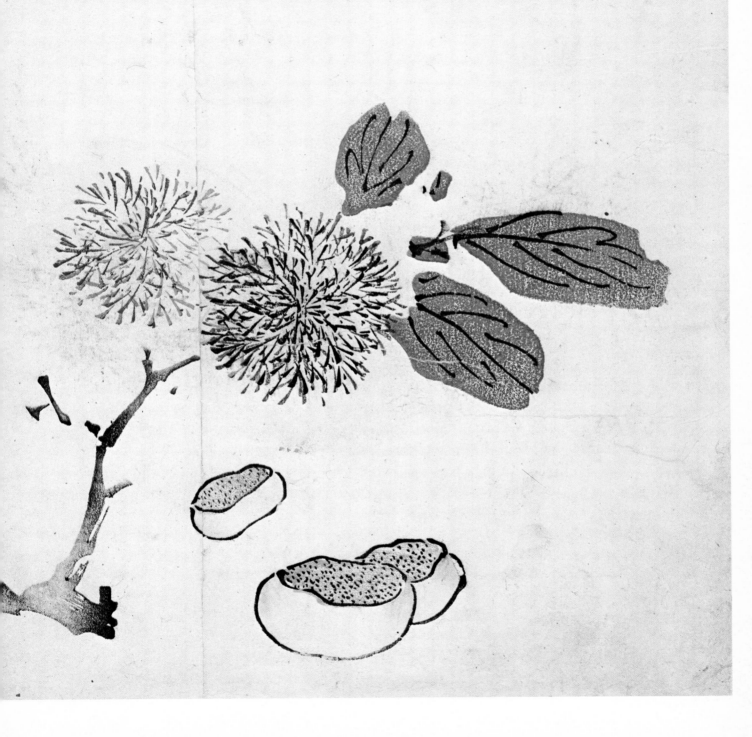

BRANCHES OF PLUM TREE AND CAMELLIA

An incompletely printed plate: the red and yellow of the flowers is absent. This plate is signed Chen Ts'ouen-ta; it is also probably from an early edition.

"Have the concern of a mother for her new-born son. A mother carefully seeks to guess at all her son's wants; her guesses are generally right. A woman has never needed to learn how to bring up children before she marries. A single family whose members help each other with affection, brings the whole nation to practise charity by its example. A single family whose members are polite and condescending between themselves, makes politeness and deference flourish among all citizens. The licentious life and perversity of one man can sow insurrection and disorder in a whole people. This is how great the influence of virtue or vice can be! The adage says: *One word ruins an affair; one man strengthens the State.*"

"The wise man treats the people in his house properly; he can then instruct his fellow citizens. His conduct towards everyone is without reproach; he governs all the people of the empire. The wise man fulfils his duties as a father, son, elder brother or younger brother in an exemplary fashion; people will imitate him. If the prince honours his parents, the people will practise filial devotion. If the prince respects his elders, the people will practise respect of their elders. If the prince is compassionate to orphans, the people will do the same. Thus the wise prince has a rule for judging."

"Do not do to inferiors anything that you would ˌnot have your superiors do to you, nor to your superiors anything that you would not have your inferiors do to you. Do not do to others who follow you anything which you would not have those who precede you do to you, nor to those who precede you anything that you would not have those who follow you do to you. Do not do to those who are on your left anything that you would not have those who are on your right do to you, nor to those on your right anything which you would not have those on your left do to you. This is called a rule for judgment. And he who holds the reins of government must, because of his dignity, be on his guard. If he commits a fault, everyone will lavish insult on him."

BIRD ON A BRANCH

This plate should be studied in conjunction with the one following it. It clearly illustrates the difference between the early editions of the Studio of the Ten Bamboos and subsequent editions which were printed with new types of wood. Rigorous draftsmanship and mastery of execution make this one of the most remarkable works of its kind.

THE CONSTANT MIDDLE

We call middle *that which does not lean to either side, and* constant *that which does not change. The middle is the direct way for all men, and constancy the invariable law which governs them.*

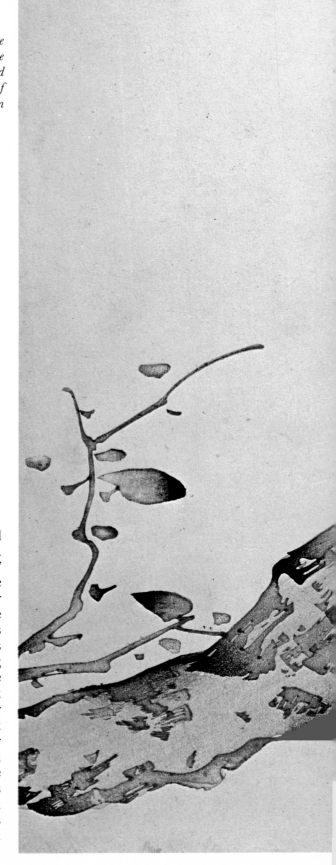

"The law that Heaven has put in the heart of man is called natural law. The observation of natural law is called the way. Teaching is called repairing the way, illuminating in mens' hearts the rule of action that passion has snuffed out. We are never allowed to swerve from the rule of our actions, even for a moment; if we were allowed to err, there would be no more rule. For this reason the wise man takes care and pays attention, even when he sees nothing that requires his vigilance; he fears and trembles, even when he hears nothing that frightens him. For him, nothing is more open than the most hidden secrets of his heart; and nothing more manifest than the smallest marks. Therefore, he watches carefully over that which only he knows, over his thoughts and his most intimate feelings. When no feeling of joy, anger, sadness or pleasure arises in the soul, we say that it is balanced. When these feelings are born in the soul without going beyond the correct measure, we say that they are in harmony. Harmony is the general law of all that is done in the universe. When balance and harmony reach their highest degree, everything is in its place in heaven and on earth; the peoples breed and develop in happiness."

BIRD ON A ROCK

This print comes from a later edition, the wood-carving having been modeled on that used in the preceding plate. From the nature of the workmanship it can be seen that two engravers were involved in its preparation: the difference of style between the bird and the bamboo branches is quite striking.

"The virtuous man stays on the Constant Middle; he who is not virtuous strays from it. Regarding the Constant Middle, the virtuous man never strays from it, because he is virtuous; he who is not virtuous, avoids and fears nothing, because he is vicious. To remain in the Constant Middle is the highest perfection. Few men are capable of remaining there long. The way of virtue is not followed; I know. Wise men seek to do too much and evil men not enough. It is thus that every man eats and drinks yet few know how to judge flavours. Alas, the way of virtue is not followed!"

"Each man brags of being skilful in business. Then he runs headlong and falls into nets, traps and ditches like a wild animal; no one knows how to escape. In the same way, everybody says: I know the way of virtue perfectly. Each knows how to find the Constant Way, but can only keep it up for the space of a month. A man can be wise enough to govern the empire and principalities, disinterested enough to refuse dignities with their income, brave enough to walk on naked swords, but unable to remain on the Constant Way."

"A disciple having asked Confucius what made up the strength of the soul, the Philosopher replied: 'Are you speaking of that of the inhabitants of the south or the inhabitants in the north, or of that which you should acquire? Teach with indulgence and gentleness, do not take revenge on injustices—this is the strength of soul of the inhabitants of the south. The wise man practises it constantly. To rest wearing arms, to give one's life without regret—this is the force of soul of the inhabitants of the north. Brave men practise it. The wise man is easy-going; but he does not let himself go to the stream of human passions. His steadfastness is brave. He keeps the straight middle without leaning to either side. How brave his steadfastness is! If the government is well run, he accepts a post in public life, but he is the same as in private life. How brave his steadfastness is! If the government is badly run, he remains the same until death. How brave is his steadfastness!"

PEONY

The red flower which should occupy the center of the composition has virtually disappeared; only a few pistils with some traces of pollen remain. The veins of the leaves are remarkable. A specimen in a better state of preservation is in the Musée Cernuschi in Paris.

"To closely examine the most impenetrable secrets, to do extraordinary things, just to be praised in centuries to come, is not what I want. The wise man walks the way of virtue. To remain halfway is something I cannot do. The wise man clings to the Constant Middle. If, by fleeing the world, he remains unknown, he is no sadder for it. The wise man alone is capable of arriving to this perfection. This wise man's rule of action is of widespread use, and yet remains partly hidden. The most ignorant people, men or women, can come to know it; but the greatest wise men themselves do not know it in its entirety. The least brave people, men or women, can undertake to follow it; but the greatest wise men themselves cannot make their conduct conform to it. It is thus that Heaven and Earth, despite their immensity, cannot satisfy fully the desires of men, who complain of cold and of heat. When the wise man reveals the great principles of natural law, nothing in the universe can contain them. When he explains the individual principles, there is nothing more subtle under heaven."

"The sparrow-hawk flies up almost to heaven; the fish dives to the deepest depths. This means that natural law manifests itself in the highest and lowest regions. The wise man's rule of action, as to its first principles, can be found in the heart of the most common people. Its furthest limits reach those of heaven and earth. It is not permitted to stray from the way of virtue."

"The rule of action is close to man. If someone made a rule which was far from man, it could not be considered as a rule. He who makes the helve of an axe has a model by him, which is the helve of the axe he already uses. He takes a helve to make another helve. Although the model is nearby, the worker who only inspects it obliqueely, judges that it is not enough like the wood intended to make a new helve. The law of our actions or natural law is even nearer to us; it is innate in us. The wise man shapes man by man, by means of natural law, which is in the heart of man; he merely corrects his faults. He applies himself seriously to the practice of virtue, measures others with the same measure as himself, and hardly ever leaves the way of perfection. He avoids doing to others what he would not have others do to him."

PLUM TREE FLOWERS

The colors have almost entirely disappeared, leaving only the outline of the branch with the stalks which were intended to bear the leaves, and also the outlines of the flowers with their pistils.

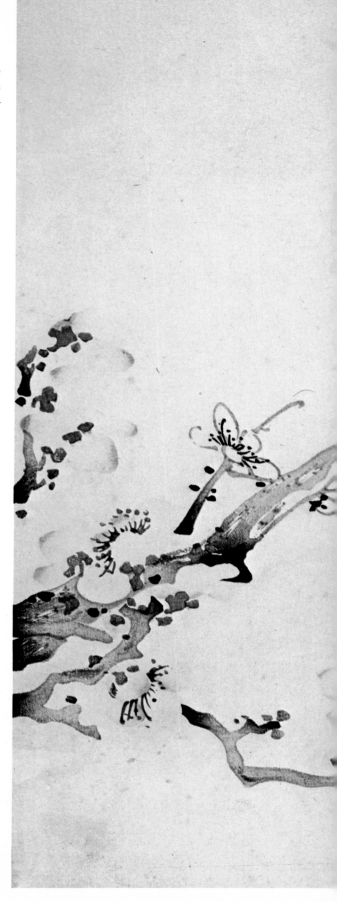

"The wise man observes four main laws; I, Confucius, have not yet been able to observe a single one. I have not yet been able to render to my father the duty that I demand from my son, nor to my prince the duty that I demand from my subjects, nor to my elder brother the duty that I demand from my younger brother; I have not yet been able to do first to my friend what I demand from him towards me. Is it not a perfectly wise man who, in the practise of ordinary virtues and in everyday conversations, tries to avoid the least faults, who always fears to promise more than he can keep, and tries to make his words suit his actions, and his actions his words?"

"In the ceremonies in honour of ancestors, relatives sat on the left and on the right, in an order corresponding to the ancestors' tables. The main assistants were placed by order of dignity; in this way the different classes of dignitaries were distinguished. Ministers were placed by order of office; in this way the different levels of virtue and capacity were distinguished. After the offerings, when the assembly had been served drinks, the lowest served those who were above them; this was an honour accorded to the lower classes. At the banquet that followed, those taking part were ranked by the colour of their hair. The perfection in filial duty was to occupy the same places as the ancestors, carry out the same ceremonies, sing the same songs, respect those they had honoured, love those they had loved, to be as dutiful to them after their death as during their lifetime, as much after they had passed on as when they were present."

28

宮錦清班

吳彬

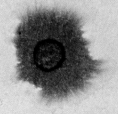

BUTTERFLY ON FLOWERY BRANCH

This plate is probably from a later edition of the Studio of the Ten Bamboos. The bouquet of flowers as well as the butterfly are not the work of the same engraver as the preceding plates; in fact the differences between them are quite striking.

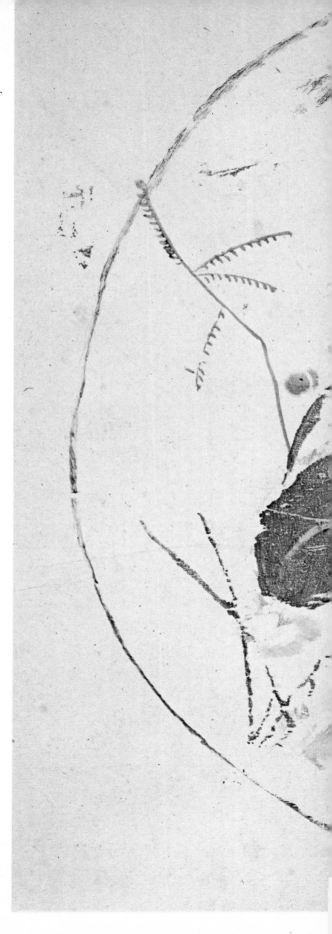

"The wise man regulates his conduct according to the condition in which he finds himself; he desires nothing outside his condition. In riches and honours he acts as is proper for a rich and honoured man. In poverty and abjection, he acts as is proper for a poor and despised man. In the midst of barbarians from the west or south, he acts is proper in the midst of these barbarians. In unhappiness and sickness, he acts as is proper in unhappiness and sickness. Always and everywhere the wise man has what is sufficient for him, that is his virtue. In a high rank, he does not get angry with his inferiors; in a low rank, he does not seek the favour of the great. He makes himself perfect, asks nothing from anyone; in addition, he never complains. He does not complain of Heaven, he does not accuse men. The wise man does not stray from the one way. He waits quietly for providence to dispose. He who is not virtuous runs after fortune over cliffs."

"Your wife and your children go together like lute and lyre. Your brothers of all ages live in harmony and are joyful together; they keep good order in your family and fill your wife and children with joy. How full of content are the father and mother. In a family, the father and mother occupy the first rank; they are above and at a distance from others. The wife, the children, the brothers of all ages occupy the second rank; they are below and near us. Begin by making good order between the wife, the children and the brothers, and by the way make the parents happy—is this not to go far leaving from a nearby place, to climb the mountain starting at its foot?"

BAMBOO AND PINE BRANCH

Quite a remarkable plate, executed by the hand of a master; one of the finest in the entire album. It is from the first edition; moreover, like the others, it is probably incomplete.

"Similar customs were adopted by princes, knights, and even scholars and men of the people. Thus if the father was a knight and the son a simple scholar, the son gave his father a knight's funeral and the offerings of a scholar. If the father was a simple scholar and the son a great knight, the son gave his father the funeral of a scholar and the offerings of a great knight. The custom of one year's mourning spread to the knights who adopted it. The custom of three years mourning spread as far as the emperor. The period of mourning for a father or a mother became the same for everybody, without distinction of rank. How great was the filial devotion of Ou Wang and Chou Noung! They followed the projects of their father and continued them admirably. In spring and autumn, they cleaned and prepared the ancestors' hall; they set out in order the objects and clothes that their fathers used; they offered them dishes and fruits in season."

"The laws common to all men are five in number; three virtues help to observe them. The five general laws are those which govern the relationship between prince and subject, between father and son, between husband and wife, between elder brother and younger brother, between companions or friends. The three virtues necessary to all men are prudence, humanity and strength. Their common quality, in order not to be sterile, is to be true and sincere. Some men possess the five great moral laws at birth; others receive them from teaching from others; others acquire them by laborious searching. However they are got, they are always the same. Some observe the five moral laws without any difficulty; others with great difficulty; others only by great effort. The final result is the same for all."

殘梢
行一

LAUGHING THRUSH ON A CAMELLIA BRANCH IN THE SNOW

This plate is complete, despite the pallid tone of the colors. This is due to the age of the print and also to the effect of exposure to the light. This print is from an early edition.

"He who loves to learn will soon acquire the virtue of prudence. He who makes the effort will soon acquire the virtue of humanity. He who knows how to blush will soon acquire the virtue of strength. To know these three things, that is to learn with ardour, to make efforts, to blush at what is evil, is to know the means of self-perfection, to know the art of governing men. To know the art of governing men, is to know how to rule the people of the empire. Whoever governs the empire must observe nine laws; these are: he must make himself perfect, respect wise men, cherish his dear ones, honour knights, keep at one with the feelings of the lower knights, give parternal help to lower subjects, attract all kinds of workers, welcome foreigners with good will, love the feudal princes. If he perfects himself, he offers his subjects a model of virtue in his person. If he respects wise men, he will never be unsure of himself. If he loves his dear ones, the relatives on his father's side of one generation before him, they will be not unhappy. If he is at one with his officers, they in return will be zealous in their service. If he loves the feudal princes he will be loved throughout the empire."

"The perfect wise man alone under the sun is capable of developing and deploying completely his natural qualities. Being able to develop and deploy his natural qualities, he can, by his example and teaching, make other men completely develop and deploy their natural qualities. Then, he can, by wise rules, make all things serve man according to the full spread of their natural qualities.

Being able to make all things serve man according to the full spread of their natural qualities, he can help Heaven and Earth teach and preserve human beings. Being able to help Heaven and Earth teach and preserve human beings, he can be associated with Heaven and Earth."

BRANCH OF CHERRY TREE

This print is probably from the same studio as No 8, and must have been produced by the same artist. The green patches on the outline of the leaves detract considerably from the fine quality of the rest of the plate. Whereas in the other plates the veins of the leaves are shown in black, here they are green.

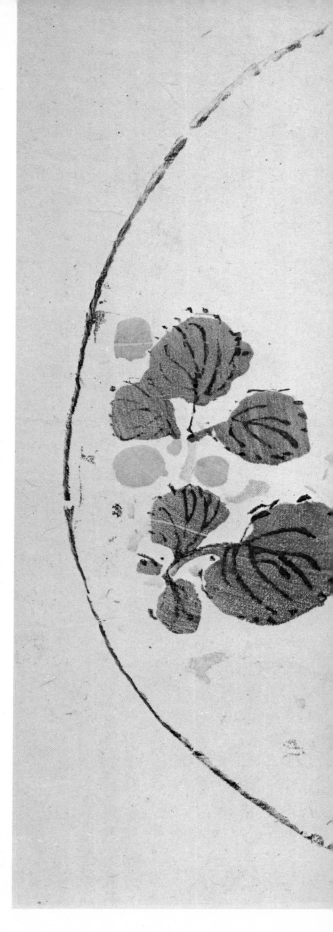

"True perfection is the work of heaven; to make it shine within oneself is the work and duty of a man. He who is naturally perfect, who has received from Heaven and always kept all virtue intact, reaches the goal without effort, follows the right way without thinking, remains easily in the correct way; this is the true wise man. He who perfects himself, embraces what is right and good, and clings to it with all his strength. He studies diligently, goes to the bottom of explanations, meditates attentively, distinguishes clearly what is good and carries it out seriously. There are things that he does not study; but what he does study, he does not abandon, even if the knowledge does not come to him. There are things that he does not mediate on; but those things on which he reflects, he does not abandon, even if he does not find what he is looking for. There are things that he does not seek to distinguish; but those that he does seek to distinguish he does not abandon, even if he cannot make them out clearly. There are things that he does not do; but what he does undertake to do, he does not abandon, even if he does not do them perfectly."

"Heaven is only a point of light; taken over its whole sweep it is an immense vault where sun, moon, and stars are hung, and which covers all beings in the universe. Earth is only a handful of dust. Because of its width and depth it holds up Mount Hua, and is not burdened by this weight; it accepts rivers and seas and lets nothing escape; it holds all human beings. The mountains are only a handful of stones; taken in the whole of their expanse, they produce all sorts of plants, act as refuge for birds and animals, abound in treasures and precious minerals. The waters could be held in a spoon; taken in their immensity, they feed the great tortoises, crocodiles, dragons, fish, little tortoises; they provide many riches and resources."

BRANCH OF LYCHEE

This plate is of very high quality; it is certainly complete and extremely well preserved. The Kao You stamp is definite proof that is comes from the first edition. The vigorous outlines of the veins, together with the ornamental detail and plasticity of the fruit, is evidence of the engraver's mastery of his art.

"Goodness constitutes human beings because every human being is good; and the way, the natural law, leads naturally to man. Goodness is the beginning and end of human beings. There is no human being who is not really good. For this reason, the wide man puts perfection above everything. True virtue does not only make perfect the man who possesses it, but it also makes perfect all things. What makes man perfect is the virtue of humanity without which man is not really man; what makes exterior things perfect is prudence, which discerns and applies the convenient means of reaching the proposed goal. These two virtues are gifts of nature, Through them, man embraces both the interior and the exterior, he perfects himself and all that is outside of himself. The property of discerning is to consult circumstances to exercise these two virtues."

"After these men, who are naturally perfect, come those who perfect a defective nature. A defective nature can become perfect. As soon as perfection appears, it becomes manifest; it shines, it exercises an influence on men and things, it changes them, it transforms them. Only he who is perfect below Heaven has the power to carry out these transformations. A truly perfect man can know the future. When a new dynasty is about to arrive, is is always announced by happy portents. When a dynasty is about to disappear, animals and inanimate things make bad omens. One sees certain signs on the milfoil and on the tortoise, certain movements in the limbs of a man's body. At the approach of a happy or unhappy event, the truly perfect man always knows well in advance what will happen that is good or evil. He can be likened to the spirits."

38

PEONIES

This plate is one of the most beautiful in the album. The firmness of the brush-strokes is evident even after printing. The skilful use of graded shades of grey and black in the leaves gives the impression of relief. It is quite possible that this plant might be from the same edition as Nos 4, 6, 7, 9 and 12.

"How great is the virtue of a perfectly wise man. It spreads beyond all boundaries, cultivates and provides for all beings. It rises above the Earth and reaches up to Heaven. In its immensity it embraces the 300 laws of morals and the three thousand rules of urbanity. When a really perfect man springs up, he will accomplish all these things. It is said that without a perfectly virtuous man, perfect virtue is not practised. The disciple of wisdom pays great attention to the virtues that nature gives, and applies himself to interrogating, to learning. He develops as many virtues as possible, and scrutinizes the most subtle points of natural law. He gives to these virtues as much lifting up and perfection as they are capable of, and always remains on the Constant Way."

"An ignorant man who wants to follows his own judgment, an inferior who wants to follow his own will, a man of our century who wants to bring back ancient customs: all these men bring trouble on themselves. No one except the Son of Heaven (the emperor) has the right to deliberate on rites, or to make laws, or to change the characters in writing. Because of this, every cart in the empire has two shafts which are at equal distance from one another; all books are written with the same letters; the conduct of all men is subject to the same laws. Although a man may have the (imperial) dignity required, if he does not have the necessary virtue, he cannot permit himself to introduce new rites or new songs. In the same way, he could not permit himself to make innovations in rites or songs, even if he did not have the required dignity, even if he had the necessary virtue. As the head of empire alone rules on these three important institutions, rites, laws and writing, he commits less errors. The institutions of the ancient emperors, although excellent, are no longer known with certitude; as they are no longer known with certitude, they have no credibility; as they have no credibility, they are not accepted by the people. Institutions made by anyone but the emperor have no authority. As they heve no authority, they do not have the confidence of the people; as they do not have the confidence of the people, they are not accepted."

BUNCH OF GRAPES

The print with the Kao You stamp belongs to the same edition as those bearing the same sign. Here again we see the same elegance in the rendering of the veins and the outline of the leaves, and the same mastery in the use of different shades of blue for the grapes.

"The goverment of a wise prince is based on the virtue of a prince and manifests itself by its effects on the whole people. If one compares it with the goverment of the founders of the three dynasties (Hia, In, Chou), one finds that it does not stray from them. If one compares it with the action of Heaven and Earth, one sees that it is not contrary to them. If one compares it to the way the spirits act, it leaves no doubt. If a great wise man were to rise up, even after one hundred generations, there would be nothing uncertain about it that he would find. Compared with the way in which the spirits act, it leaves no doubt, because a wise man knows and imitates the action of Heaven and the spirits. If a great wise man were to rise up, even after one hundred generations, he would find nothing uncertain in it, because a wise prince knows the way that man must follow. Therefore, the conduct of a wise prince will always be the model for the whole empire; his actions will always be the rule for the whole empire; he words will always be the law for the whole empire. Those who are far from him, want to be close to him; those who are close to him, never leave his presence. There, nobody hates them; here, nobody is tired of their presence. Their memory will be celebrated through the ages."

"He who possesses perfect wisdom is alone in having enough perception, intelligence, sagacity and prudence to rule his subjects; enough generosity, grandeur of soul, affability and goodness to love all men; enough activity, courage, firmness and constancy to faithfully fulfil his duty; enough integrity, gravity, moderation and uprightness to keep himself from all negligence; enough order and continuity in his actions, enough care and vigilance in his affairs, to know how to be discerning. Perfect virtue embraces all things in its immensity; it is deep and springs up like an inexhaustible source. The wise man makes it appear according to circumstances. It is immense and universal like Heaven; deep and inexhaustible like the sea. The wise man shows himself and everybody respects him; he speak and everybody believes him; he acts and everybody is happy. Everywhere that ships and transports can reach, everywhere where the strength of man reach, wherever the vault of Heaven stretches, wherever the Earth bears human beings, wherever the sun and the moon spread their light, wherever frost and dew form, everything that has spirit and life, venerates and loves the wise man. Therefore, he is compared to Heaven."

BRANCH OF POMEGRANATE TREE

This plate is from the same edition as Nos 8 and 11. The colors are pale and relatively poorly matched. Compared to the preceding plate, it is obviously from a later edition.

"Only the truly perfect man is capable of determining the five great laws of social relations, of establishing the basis of human society, the virtues of humanity, justice, urbanity, prudence and sincerity, and of knowing how Heaven and Earth produce and keep all things. And what help does he find beside himself? He achieves all this by himself, without any outside help. His virtue is very diligent, his science very deep, his action as immense as Heaven. He who is not himself very perspicacious, very prudent, extremely versed in the knowledge of natural values, can he know the perfectly wise man? The virtue of the wise man is to remain hidden; his brilliance will increase every day. On the other hand, the virtue of the vulgar man likes to be seen; it disappears little by little. The virtue of the wise man has no particular flavour; it never exites disgust; it is simple, but not devoid of ornamentation; without affectedness, but not without order."

"He who knows the closely-related means that lead far, he who knows that morals can be reformed by correcting oneself; he who knows that interior virtue manifests itself on the outside; this man can be admitted to the school of wisdom. As the fish hides at the bottom of the pool, he will be perfectly seen. If the wise man examines himself and finds himself without fault, then his heart is satisfied. The place were the wise man exercises his vigilance more than any other man, is where no one sees him, that is, in his own heart."

"'There should be nothing in your house of which you should be ashamed, even in the rooms which face to the northwest, and receive light only by the roof, and where you can be seen, if not by men, then at least by spirits. The wise man is always on his guard, even when he is at rest; he is sincere, even when he is not speaking. When he offers his stew and invites the spirits to come, he does not speak; therefore no discussion arises and all those at table imitate his respectful silence. The wise man, without giving recompenses, encourages the people; without getting irritated, he inspires fear more than the sword or the hangman. Their virtue, without shining brightly, is imitated by the feudal princes. The wise man keeps close watch over himself, and all the empire is in peace."

BAMBOO

This remarkable monochrome print is from one of the early editions. The bamboo leaves, which are drawn in a single line, and the fineness of the branches are both evidence of the same mastery as that shown in the preceding monochrome prints. Taken as a whole the work shows that a print executed in a single color often makes a stronger impression than a polychromatic print.

On entering the palace, he bowed as if the gate were too small to let him through. He never stood at the middle of the entrance; in walking he avoided to put his foot on the threshold. When he passed near the prince's throne, between the door and the interior separation, Confucius showed a feeling of respect so deep that the look on his face became changed and his gait embarassed, even if the prince were not there; he seemed at a loss for words. He went up to the great hall, holding up his gown, his body bowed and holding his breath as if he could no longer breathe. On leaving, as soon as he had come down the first level, his face took back its usual look; he appeared affable and joyful. Arriving at the lower levels, he hastened his step, holding his hands joined and his arms lifted a little like a bird with its wings stretched. On returning to his place, he appeared to be experiencing a feeling of respectful fear.

When Confucius was commanded by the prince to receive guests, the look on his face seemed changed and his gait embarassed. To hail guests on their arrival, he joined his hands and held his body stiff, turning only his joined hands to right and left to the guests who were at his sides; his gown remained well adjusted at front and back. Bringing the guests in he walked with a quick step, holding his hands joined and his arms a little stretched, like the wings of a bird. After a guest had left, he always warned the prince who was at the gate, where he himself had taken the guest. He would say to him: "the guest is no longer looking back, therefore the prince ca return to his suite."

MANDARINS AND PERSIMMON

The mandarins are arranged in a blue dish, the fruit of the persimmon on a brown plinth. Comparing this plate with prints from other editions, one can clearly see that it is probably from one of the earlier editions.

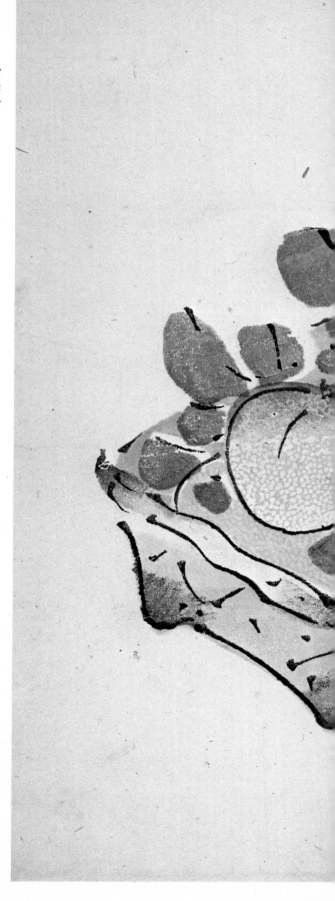

When Confucius presented himself as an envoy at a foreign court, he held his prince's tablet in both hands, his body bowed, as if he did not have the strength to hold it up; he lifted the tablet as if he were saluting, that is, to head-height; he lowered it as if he were offering an object, that is, at breast height. He had the look of a man who is trembling with fear. He hardly lifted his feet when walking, as if he were walking in someone's footsteps. When he offered the foreign prince his master's presents, he was affable and joyful. When he offered his own presents during a private visit, he was even more affable.

This great man did not wear a collar with a blue-red edge, because this was the collar for days of abstinence, nor did he wear a collar with a red-black edge, as this was the collar worn for the second and third year of three-year mourning. He never wore clothes of pink colour, not of violet colour, because they were not among the five basic colours, and because they were too like women's clothes. During the summer heat, under a tunic of hemp in a loose material, he wore another tunic to hide his body perfectly. In winter he wore a black tunic over a lined tunic in black lambskin, or a white tunic over a tunic lined with white doeskin, or a yellow tunic over a tunic lined with yellow fox fur. The fur-lined jacket that he ordinarily wore was long; but the right sleeve was shorter than the left, so that the right hand would be more free to work. The clothes heavily lined with fox or marten fur were used in his home.

BAMBOOS

This plate, which is printed in two colors, is extraordinarily subtle. The engraver has skilfully arranged the grey on the leaves so that the viewer is made to feel that they are being moved by the same wind that is stirring the waves in the stream.

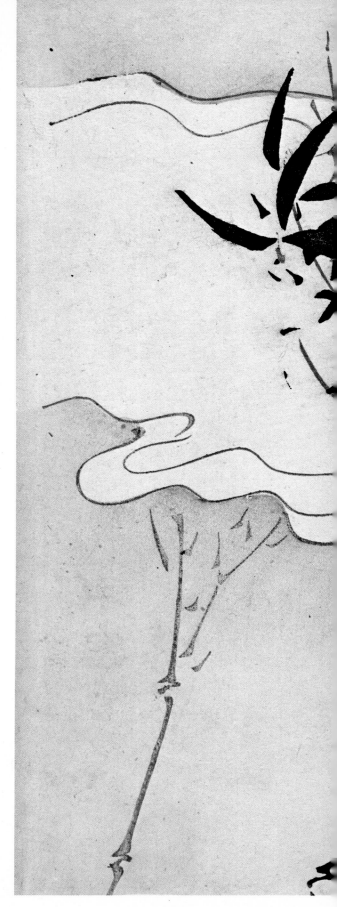

Confucius liked his gruel to be made of very pure rice and his mincemeat to be made of very finely minced meat. He never ate mouldy gruel, nor fish or meat that was beginning to smell. He never ate a dish that had lost its colour or ordinary smell. He never ate a dish that was not properly cooked, nor a fruit that was not ripe enough. He never ate anything that had not been cut in the right way, nor anything that had not been seasoned with the right sauce. Even when meat was in plenty, he never took more meat than vegetables. The amount of fermented drink that he took was never measured, but he never drank as much as to cloud his head. He never took fermented liquor or dried meat that had been bought, for fear that they were not clean. He always had ginger at his table. He did not eat to excess. He did not keep more than three days meat that he had offered to his departed relations. Past three days they would not have eaten it.

When the prince sent him a prepared dish, he tasted it on a conveniently laid mat, without offering it to the dead. When the prince sent him raw meat, he cooked it and offered it to the dead. When the prince gave him a live animal, he fed it. When he ate in the palace at the prince's side, at the moment when the latter offered dishes to the dead, Confucius tasted the dishes from a feeling of modesty, as if he had not been the prince's guest, but only the cook. When he was sick and the prince came to visit him, he turned his head to the west, after having put his bed by the window which faced south; he put on court clothes and put his official belt over them. When the prince called him to the palace, he went on foot without waiting for the carriage to be drawn up. At the death of one of his friends, if their were no relations to take care of the funeral, he used to say: "I will look after the service." When he received presents from his friends, if they were carriages or horses, he made no sign of thanks, unless it was meat offered to the dead.

PLUM TREE FLOWERS AND BAMBOOS

The last of the series here presented, this is one of the most beautiful of the colored prints. It is complete, and is engraved with the same mastery as shown in the preceding work. The workmanship displayed in the rendering of the leaves makes it clear that these last plates were from the same studio.

Laid down to rest, he did not stretch like a dead man. At home, his bearing was not too serious. When he saw a man wearing mourning, even if it was an intimate friend, he looked compassionate through politeness. If he saw a man in official dress or a blind man, even in private, he never went without showing him a sign of respect. When he was in his carriage and he saw a man in mourning, he put his hands on the window ledge of the carriage, and greeted him with a bowing of the head. If he met a man carrying census tablets, he saluted him in the same way. If a great banquet was prepared for him, he stood up and thanked the master of the house. When it thundered and the wind blew hard, the look on his face witnessed his respect for an angry Heaven.

When he got into his carriage he held his body straight and took in his hand the rope used to pull himself up. In the carriage, he did not look back, never spoke precipitately and never pointed.

When a bird sees a menacing man, it flies off, turns in circles and then sets down again. Confucius said: "How the pheasant, on the bridge, in the mountains, knows how to choose its time to fly off and set down again. If a bird can see every little movement, should a man come and go without examining himself or deliberating?"

冬梅
沈存德

Plates from the
Kaempfer Series

Selected texts from
Meng - T'seu

BIRTH WISH

**Do not take away the one-day beauty,
the pomegranate picked before the
house is sufficient!**

*The flowers and fruits of the pomegranate tree symbolize the
wish for the birth of a son. The cricket is the symbol of life
and death eternally renewed. The day-lily, called "one-day
beauty", is a yellow lily, whose pretty flowers last only a
day. Pregnant women wore them at their belt if they wanted
to give birth to a son.*

ENTRETIENS

"The wise man aspires to perfection, the
common man to wellbeing; the wise man sets
himself to observing the laws, and the common
man attempts to attract favours to himself."

"If your parents fall into error, warn them
with great gentleness. If you see that they are not
going to follow your advice, double your respect
and repeat your remonstrances. Even if they
mistreat you, do not resent it."

"During your parents'life, never journey far. If
you travel, let it be in a known direction so that
they know where you are. You must often
remind yourself of your parents' age, to rejoice
in their long life, and to fear that they should not
die."

"A piece of rotten wood could not be sculpted; a midden wall could not be plastered. What
is the use of telling Tsai Yu off? Once I believed
that when I had heard a man speak his
conduct corresponded to his words. Now when I
hear a man speak, I then look to see if his
actions correspond to his words. It is Tsai Yu
who made me change my rule of judgment."

BUTTERFLIES ON A BRANCH OF MISTLETOE

**I have found so much gold in the
shrubbery!
It's no secret:
The mistletoe fruits are already ripe.**

*This form of well-whishing was probably used by a suitor to
his fiancée to explain his desire to marry the young lady.
Mistletoe is a parasite growing on the branches of fruit trees,
mainly apple trees, pear trees and cherry trees. In this form,
the fruit tree is most likely a cherry tree, the symbol of spring.
Mistletoe symbolizes togetherness. The butterflies, according
to some authors, could mean the hope of procreation.*

"In a village of ten families there are certainly
men to whom nature has given, as to me, the
gifts of faithfulness and sincerity; but there are
none, who like me, practise to have knowledge
of these virtues."

"Yen Hu Way's wisdom was great! He lived in
a miserable street with only a basket of food and
a spoonful of water to drink. Another, seeing
him so poorly off, would have experienced
intolerable sorrow. Hu Way was always happy."

"Meditate and engrave in your memory the
precepts of wisdom, learn without ever reaching
surfeit, teach without ever tiring of it; can these
three virtues be found in me? What I fear is not
applying myself to the practise of virtue, of not
seeking to have explained to me what I have to
learn, of not being able to accomplish what I
know to be my duty, and of not being able to
correct my faults."

"Always make yourself follow the way of
virtue; stay on this path; never stray from the
way of perfection; take the six liberal arts for
your relaxation: urbanity, archery, the art of
driving a cart, writing and mathematics."

飜得黃金
真纍落
莫教錯認
是琵琶
　亮先氏

THE WISH OF LONG LIFE

**The Queen Mother of the West sowed
them
Three thousand years ago,
And only today
Do they offer their fruit.**

The Queen Mother of the West is a popular Chinese religious figure. The cicada symbolizes the cycle of life and death. The two symbols are of great importance in the ancestors' cult, once observed by every Chinese according to rites and duties imposed by family piety. One of the most important duties that existed in China since time immemorial, was to wish long life at every opportunity and reassure the person celebrating his birthday, that after his death his memory and worship would be carefully respected.

"If it were a good thing to seek to amass riches, even if to do this meant fulfilling the office of the valet who holds the whip, I would do it. But as long as it is not a good thing to seek them, I will follow the object of my desires—wisdom."

"Even if a wise man were reduced to eating gross food, to drinking water and sleeping with his head on his arm, he keeps his joy amid all these privations. The riches and dignity obtained by evil ways seem to me like clouds that float in the air; they do not make man happy."

"If I were travelling with two companions, one virtuous and the other evil, both would be my masters. I would examine that what the first had that was good, and I would imitate it; I would try to correct in myself the faults I saw in the other."

60

WISH FOR A LONG LIFE

**The crysanthemum ignores the cold
and flowers gorgeously in the middle of
autumn;
he is at one with the Master of the
Eastern hedge
who has since become his friend.**

*The bird is probably a Thsio—a species that was a bird of
good omen to the Chinese and always brought joy. It is
perched on an apple tree branch (the May tree), which is
covered with mistletoe, symbolizing togetherness and
friendship. Four crysanthemum flowers, the symbol of
November, probably symbolize the period of time completed.*

"It has not been given to me to see a man of
extraordinary wisdom; if I see only a truly wise
man, I will be happy. It has not been given to
me to see a man without reproach; if I only see a
man of constant will, I will be happy enough. He
who has nothing and pretends to have
something, who is empty and seeks to look full,
who has few things and seeks to make a great
show of his splendour, cannot be constant."

"There are perhaps men who go into under-
takings blindly; I do not act this way. After
having heard a lot, I choose and make good of
what I have learnt that is useful; after having
seen a lot, I engrave in my memory that which I
have noted. I am one of those who comes
immediately after the great wise men whose
knowledge is innate."

"He who is over-polite, is tiring;he who is
over-circumspect is fearful; he who is brave
beyond measure causes disorder; he who is frank
beyond measure, offends by too pressing advise.
If the prince fulfils his duties with zeal towards
his parents and ancestors, family piety will
flourish among the people. If the prince does not
abandon his old servants and friends, the people
will follow his example."

62

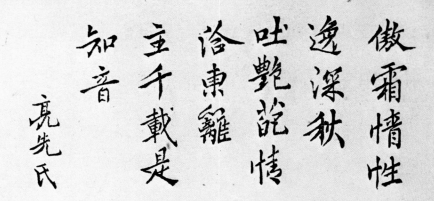

傲霜情性
逸深秋
吐艷兌情
涂東籬
主千載是
知音
亮先氏

SYMBOLIC COMPOSITION

Red and purple lift my soul.
Cut these scented branches;
how fresh the colours are!

A wish of happiness and harmony. Red is a joyful and fresh colour. The peony is a symbol of success, of distinction and promotion. The basket is the symbol of perfect agreement. The form of the wish was probably sent to someone who had passed exams or who had been promoted in the civil service.

"The wise man clings to the precepts of wisdom and he loves to study them. He observes them faithfully until death, and by study convinces himself of their excellence. He does not visit a country threatened by revolution; he does not remain in a State troubled by dissensions. If the empire is well governed, he shows himself, he can and he must accept an office in the interest of the emperor and the people. If the empire is badly governed, the wise man would by ashamed to have neither riches and honours."

"If, after having undertaken to build a hillock, I abandon my work when I only need one more basket of earth, it would be true to say that I have abandoned my undertaking. If, after having begun to make an embankment, I continue my work; even if I only add one basket of earth, my undertaking is progressing. If the disciple of wisdom makes efforts continually, even little at a time, he is picking up a lot; but if he stops half-way, he will lose the fruit of the work he has already accomplished."

A FORM OF WISHES FOR AN EXAM PASSED

**By the Foukien sea
the first fruits of summer
will get you a deep, rich red.**

Civil servants' promotion exams generally took place in spring. Foukien was a Chinese province situated opposite the island of Taiwan—the Foukien sea is called the Straits of Formesa today. The Chinese strawberries and the religious mint on the lychee branch on the left, form an harmonious group intended to congratulate the person who has passed exams, which give him the right to the civil servant's red clothing.

"The wise man cannot be appreciated in small things, because he cannot excel in every little detail; but he can be trusted with things of importance. Important things cannot be entrusted to the common man; but he can be appreciated in small things, because he can only excel in small things."

"Three sorts of friendship are advantageous and three sorts of friendship are damaging. Friendship with a man who speaks directly, friendship with a sincere man, friendship with a man of great knowledge, these three sorts of friendship are useful. Friendship with a man skilled in flattery, friendship with a man who speaks a lot, friendship with a man used to misleading by false appearances, these three sorts of friendship are damaging."

"There are three things that are worth loving, and three things that are damaging to love. Love of the study of ceremonies and music, love of saying well of what one has observed in others, love of making friends with many wise and virtuous men, these three things are worthwhile. Love of giving free rein to one's greed, love of losing one's time and running hither and thither, love of feasts and dishonest pleasures, these three passions are damaging."

閩海夏深
初熟子
相傳第一
狀元紅
亮先氏

CRYSANTHEMUMS AND BUTTERFLIES

**Now I no longer envy T'Ao Ts'ien
the flowers which charmed him
for those on my Eastern hedge
brave the autumn winds all alone.**

*T'ao Ts'ien was a civil servant, who, having retired from
imperial service, took up crysanthemum growing. The wishes
were probably sent to those who, after a long career, retired
or were able to take up another job that they had long sought.*

"He who applies himself to practising virtue
is on his guard against three things. In youth
when the blood and vital spirits are always in
movement, he guards himself against the
pleasures of the senses. In maturity, when the
blood and spirits are in full vigour, he avoids
quarrels. In old age, when the blood and spirits
have lost their energy, he guards against
acquisitive passion."

"The wise man respects three things. He
respects the will of Heaven, natural law, he
respects men who are eminent in virtue and
dignity; he respects the sayings of sages. The
vulgar man knows no natural law, and does not
respect it; he derides the sayings of the sages."

A FORM OF WISHES

Picked and placed in the Golden House,
the strange flowers;
the miraculous beauty of each one!
Their divine scent envelops you with
respect and happiness.

Five objects in an allegorical composition. A basket with flowers, a camelia and narcissuses, a square bronze vase decorated with soothsaying motifs from the I Ching Book of Changes, from which peonies and orchids emerge. A bronze tripod decorated with Taoist symbols, with smoke forming and a bat flying in it, is set on a wood and stone stand. In the right corner, a scent burner in the shape of a duck used in worship ceremonies, and finally, a gourd—a Taoist symbol—hanging from an upright. This form was used to wish luck and happiness.

"Those in whom the knowledge of the principles of wisdom is innate are quite superior men. In the second rank come those who have acquired this knowledge by study: and in the third rank, those who, despite their intelligence, work to acquire it. Those who are neither intelligent nor have the will to learn, form the final class of men."

"The wise man pays special attention to nine things. He applies himself to see properly what he is looking at, to listen well to what he hears; he is careful to look affable, to dress irreproachably, to be sincere in his words, to be diligent in his actions; when in doubt, he takes the trouble to ask; when he is annoyed, he thinks of the bad consequences of his anger; when faced with obtaining a property, he consults the law."

"When you see there is good to be done, use all your energy, as if you were afraid that you could never do it; when there is evil to avoid, jump back as if you had put your hand into boiling water; it is a principle that I have seen put into practise and that I learned from the ancients. Prepare in solitude to serve prince and country, practise justice, in order to spread far the influence of virtue; it is a principle that I learned from the ancients, but never yet saw followed by anyone."

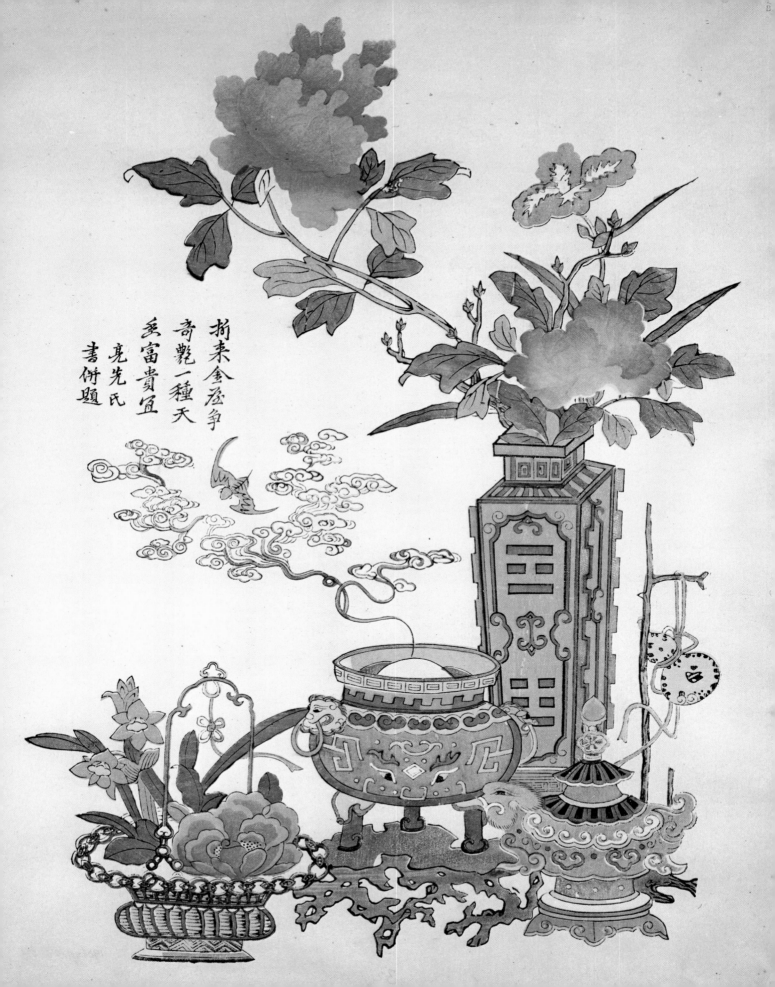

BIRD ON A POMEGRANATE TREE

**Crimson beauty like frost
spread on countless rushes.
Splashes of summer light on
the curve of the staircase.**

*The bird perched on a pomegranate branch is the wish for
the birth of a son, with a few magnolia flowers in the left
corner. Red is a symbol of joy, magnolia is the February
flower. This was a form of wishes used in springtime or at
the birth of a son.*

"When one does nothing but drink and eat all day, without applying one's mind to an occupation, it is difficult to become virtuous! Are there not tablets and chess? Better play games than do nothing at all."

"The great wise men of old, wanting to use more than the perception of their sight, made use of the compass, the angle-bracket, the spirit level and the plumb line to make squares, circles, flat surfaces and straight lines; we will always be able to use these instruments. Wanting to use more than the power of their hearing, they used six tubes to determine the five sounds; we will always be able to use these tubes. Wanting to use more than the power of their intelligence, they governed their subjects with understanding charity, and their charity spread throughout the universe."

72

SYMBOLIC COMPOSITION

The basket full of lotus flowers;
how many bunches will it need for the
wise man withdrawn from the world to
be happy?

The basket, symbol of harmony, with lily flowers, symbol of hope, a pomegranate tree branch symbol used for the birth of a boy, and lotus flowers, symbol of the Western Lands, the paradise of the Buddha Amitabha, of the popular Chinese religion. A form used for a wellearned retirement.

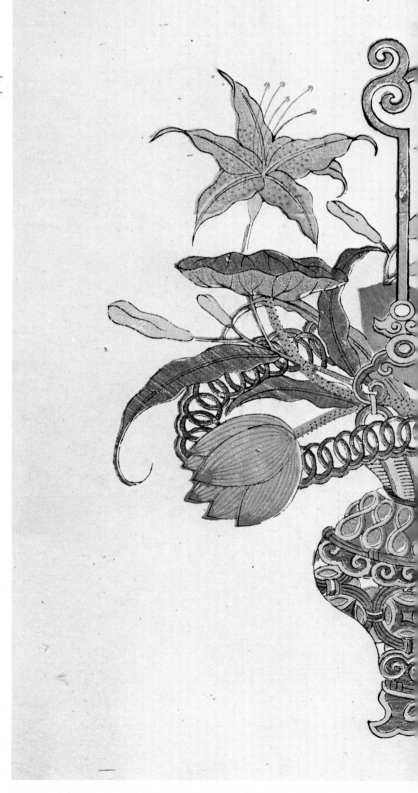

"A proverb says: 'He who wishes to build high must build on a hill or on a mountain; he who wishes to build low must build on the bed of a river or on a marsh.' Can he who in government does not apply the principles of the ancient sovereigns be called wise? A human prince alone is worthy of exercising sovereign authority. An inhuman prince who exercises sovereign authority propagates his vices among his subjects. If the prince in his councils recognizes neither right nor justice, the ministers and subjects will not recognize the authority of the laws. The prince will not let himself be led by justice, nor the officers by the laws. If the State escapes from total ruin, then it will owe it only to good luck."

74

蓮花蓮葉
滿藍筐
幾朶嬌姿
嫩六師
丁亥先製

PINE, BAMBOO AND PLUM TREE

Bamboo shoots and plum tree flowers,
their unique charm in springtime.
My hidden feelings
look like winter rushes.

Three friends, the pine tree, plum tree and bamboo tree,
symbols of long life and of winter, are also symbols of the
quality of a good man. The plum tree symbolizes a good
appearance and unshakeable independence—the plum tree
flowers before all other trees. The pine symbolized faithful
friendship which resists all trials. The bamboo is the symbol
of the application of the disciple and of the man who remains
loyal in all events. The three symbols represent the three
Chinese religions: Taoism, Buddhism and Confucianism.
The form was used to express thanks.

"The compass and the angle bracket are used for tracing circles and perfect squares. Indeed, great wise man are the most perfect models of the five virtues that man must practice towards others. The prince who seeks to fulfil his princely duties perfectly, and the citizen who wishes to perfectly fulfil his duties as a citizen, have only to imitate Iao and Chouen. He who does not serve his prince like Chouen has served Iao and is not faithful to his prince. He who does not govern like Iao, badly harms his people." "There are only two ways: the way of virtue and the way of vice. If a prince violently oppresses his people, he perishes by violent death and his kingdom is lost to his race. If he does not oppress them violently, his person is in danger and his kingdom is put at risk. After his death he will be called Blind and Cruel. His descendants will not be able to change these ignominious names, even after one hundred generations, however great their filial piety is."

SYMBOLIC COMPOSITION

**The Huns' drum threatens the flowers
and the brilliance of their splendour.
A soft wind covers them with dust,
and spreads their scent.**

A glazed basket, decorated with bamboo rushes and garnished with narcissus, red camelias and with a flowering branch. The poem is of the Hing literary type, which consists of speaking first of things foreign to the subject only to introduce the feelings that one wishes to express later. This is a description of the dawning of spring—a form of greeting used to wish happiness in the coming spring.

"He who cultivates perfectly his intelligence, knows nature and the nature of all things. He who knows nature, knows Heaven. Intelligence is the faculty of the mind with which man has gleaned the principles of all knowledge, and through which he conducts himself in all things. Nature is the grouping of all principles that intelligence naturally knows, Heaven is the principle of all principles. There is no one whose intelligence does not possess the principles of all knowledge. The way of serving Heaven is to perfectly keep intellectual faculties and to nourish within oneself the gifts of nature. The way of affirming the gifts that one has received from Heaven is to be indifferent to the subject of the length or shortness of life, and to work to perfect oneself until the end of one's career."

羯鼓催苍
光爛漫
煖玉施粉
更芳菲

丁亥宗

NEW YEAR WISHES

In the valley of frost -
I wait for spring to knock at my door
and play court to my shadows.

An allegorical composition with a box decorated with bamboo rushes and a Chinese proverb, and containing brushes, rolls of paper and a fan. In the background a bronze vase with two handles in the shape of dragons, containing camelia flowers and a plum tree branch in flower. The laquered tripod with handles in the shape of horses was probably used as an ashtray. The little box on the right held essences for burning. In front of it, a pomegranate in a bowl. The plum tree, the January tree, symbolizes the beginning of the year.

"Before speaking or acting, the wise man does not renew his resolution to be sincere or brave; he says or does what it is simply convenient to say or do, according to the circumstances, and he is always sincere and brave, he practises virtue naturally, without effort, without having to think of it. That man is truly great whose heart is still as on his day of birth, free of all evil desire, loving only virtue."

"If someone loves others and is not loved in return, he should examine himself to see if his charity is perfect. If someone governs others and cannot rule their conduct, he should examine himself to see if his prudence is perfect. If someone is polite and receives nothing in return, he should examine himself to see if his respect for others is perfect. If someone does not reach the goal he has set himself in his actions, he should examine himself and look for the cause of his failure in his own conduct. Let a prince be perfect himself, and the Empire will be his. A prince loved by the great families will be loved by the subjects of the whole kingdom. A prince loved by all the subjects of the kingdom will be loved by the inhabitants of the whole empire. His virtues and teaching will spread everywhere between the four seas with the speed of a torrent."

EXPRESSION OF THANKS

**The Jade of the Ching mountain
casts the shadow into confusion.
The peach trees in flower,
their beauty charms me.**

The Hoang Niao bird, which has yellow feathers, and green or partly black wings. It is the size of a sparrow and has a very soft chirp; the male and the female always fly together, and stop singing at the 8th Chinese moon (September-October). It is sitting on a pomegranate branch. The poem alludes to an ancient story, which praises the faithful servant, who did not hesitate to have his legs cut off to prove the truth of his words. The Chinese used the word "jade" to indicate any precious stone, whereas in the West it means natural silicate of aluminium and calcium, the colour of which varies from a whitish olive to dark green.

"It is impossible to speak to a man who does serious harm to himself. It is impossible to do nothing with a man who lets himself go. To blame what is honest and just is called seriously harming oneself. To pretent to not be able to be constantly perfect nor to observe justice, is to let oneself go. Perfection is the quiet house, justice the straight way of man. To leave empty and not live in the peaceful house, to abandon and not follow the narrow way is deplorable! The way of virtue is near us; it is the natural law which is engraved in our hearts; some go far to seek it. It is easy to practice virtue; some make it difficult. Let every man love his parents and respect those who are above him; order will then reign in the whole universe."

82

SYMBOLIC COMPOSITION

A bouquet of flowers and the shadow
which reflects its beauty on the ground.
The dazzling light of the peach tree.

*This is an allegorical composition with chrysanthemums in a
bronze vase, painted rolls and a dead branch in a richly
decorated receptacle. The tripod, the closed book and the open
book indicate that this formula was sent on the occasion of a
successful examination.*

"It is useful to seek the good that we find,
when we seek it and lose it, when we neglect it.
This good is inside us; it is virtue. There is no
point in looking for good whose following is
subjected to certain rules, and whose gaining
depends on the will of Heaven. This goodness is
outside us. In us we have the principles of all
knowledge. The greatest happiness of all is seeing, when we examine ourselves, that nothing is
missing in our own perfection. If a man tries to
love others as himself, the perfection that he
seeks is close by him."

"A subject who does not have the trust of his
prince can never govern the people; the people
will not trust him. To earn the trust of a prince,
there is a way to follow. He who does not have
the trust of his friends, will not have that of his
prince. To win the trust of friends, there is a way
of conduct. He who does not satisfy his parents
will not have the trust of his friends. To satisfy
parents, there is a way of conduct. He who, in
examining himself, recognizes that he is not
applying himself seriously to gaining the
perfection that is given to each man will not
satisfy his parents. To gain natural perfection,
there is a way to follow. He who does not
distinguish properly what is honest and good
will not gain natural perfection. Natural
perfection is the work of Heaven; to apply
oneself to gaining natural perfection is the work
of man. A completely perfect man will always
earn trust. An imperfect man has never been
able to earn it."

BIRD ON A FLOWERY BRANCH

**The moon is bright
in the cool autumn air.
Standing near the window
I gaze upon the hibiscus.
Purity.**

*This marvellous print, which is remarkably composed and
colored, is of a sort which used to be sent on birthdays or at
the New Year; it is one of the finest in the series. The
hibiscus, which symbolized wisdom and austerity, was a
favorite flower of the Chinese.*

"Nothing exists that has not been desired or
ordered by Heaven. We must accept with
submission what it desires and orders directly.
Only the things that happen without man
attracting them are ordered directly by Heaven.
It neither wants nor orders other things in a
direct way and often man must try to avoid
them. For this reason, he who has a good idea of
heavenly providence, does not stand at the foot
of a crumbling wall, so as to not attract a death
that Heaven does not directly want. The death
of he who ends his days in the accomplishment
of heavenly duties is directly ordered by Heaven.
The death of the criminal who perishes in chains
is not."

BEST WISHES FOR A LONG LIFE

Her peerless beauty
is praised everywhere
and it is amongst us
that she spreads her scent.

*A butterfly, the symbol of harmonious understanding, is fly-
ing around a rose branch in bloom. This greeting card was
probably sent in connection with a birthday.*

"The principal fruit of goodness is filial piety.
The main fruit of justice is condescention to
elder brothers. The principal fruit of wisdom is
the knowledge and constant practise of these
two virtues. The principal fruit of urbanity is to
rule and crown these two virtues. The principal
fruit of music is to make them pleasant. Once
pleasant, they will develop. How can they be
stopped in their development? As they can no
longer be stopped, they appear in all the
movements of our feet and our hands, without
our noticing."

88

競誇天下春
雙艷獨占人
間第一条
石宗氏

BEST WISHES

**The plum tree and the camellia
live in the cold valley;
their feelings are secret.**

*Three periods in the life of a lotus flower: bud, bloom and
faded flower, symbolizing the passage of time. The bird is
eating seeds in the lotus pods. This greeting formula was
sent to those celebrating a birthday.*

"If virtuous men train those who are not
virtuous, and if capable men train those who are
not capable, the youngest will be happy to have
fathers and elders who are capable and virtuous.
If virtuous men pay no attention to those who
are not virtuous, if capable men pay no attention
to those who are not capable, there will be
hardly an inch in distance between virtuous and
capable men, but without any pity, and the
others will be neither virtuous nor capable."

90

ALLEGORICAL COMPOSITION

The lotus pods and the young cut flowers are placed in an enamelled stemmed bowl. The lotus is the symbol of wisdom and purity. This formula was sent on the occasion of a successful examination.

"The disciple of wisdom advances continuously along the true way, that is, by degrees. He wants to possess wisdom as if it were naturally in him. When it becomes natural in him, he keeps it peacefully. When he keeps it peacefully, he has an abundant treasure. When he has an abundant treasure, he can delve into it and use it on all occasions; he is always at the source, as wisdom has become natural in him and seems to flow from the source. For this reason the disciple of wisdom wishes to possess it as perfectly as if it were natural in him. He who cultivates wisdom learns all its precepts and exposes them clearly, not to show great erudition, but to return subsequently to his knowledge and summarize it."

GREETINGS

When they enter the house
oh my loved one
these marvellous flowers
greet my dwelling.

A branch of the pomegranate in bloom, in a richly decorated bronze vase. A box which was used to store essences for burning, a blue ashtray, a half-open painted roll, a gourd and a seal complete this composition, which served as a means of wishing a newborn son a brilliant career.

"If at first it seems that you can receive a thing, and then that you cannot, when you receive it you will be missing the virtue of integrity. If at first it seems that you can give a thing, and then that you cannot, in giving it you will violate the rules of charity. If at first it seems that you can sacrifice your life, and then that you cannot, in confronting death, you will be missing the virtue of strength."

"The wise man is different from other men because he keeps the virtues that nature has put in his heart. He keeps charity and urbanity in his heart. A charitable man loves others; a polite man respects others. He who loves others is always loved; he who respects others is always respected. Suppose there is someone here who treats me in a rough and rude way. If I am wise, I will go into myself and say: Certainly, I have lacked in charity and urbanity to this man. If not, would he have treated me in a rough and rude way? I examine myself and see that I have lacked neither gentleness nor urbanity. However, he continues to treat me in a rough and rude way. As a wise man, I examine myself again and say: To be sure I have not done for this man all that I could have done. By examining myself, I find no lack of kindness to reproach myself. Nonetheless, this man continues to treat me in a rough and rude way. As a wise man, I say to myself: He is mindless. Is a man like him different from a man deprived of his reason? Should I torment myself over a man without reason?"

奇葩帶露移來玩開向
名園入錦圍 亮先氏書

GREETINGS

**After winter, the spring returns;
hope and be patient.**

A pair of birds on the branch of a cherry tree; two camellias in the right corner complete this composition. These three symbols were meant to assure the newlywed couple that their offspring would be numerous.

"A man from Ts'i had a wife and a concubine with whom he lived. When he went out, he always gorged himself with wine and meat. On coming home his wife asked him who it was he had eaten and drunk with. To hear him, it was with rich and honourable men. His wife spoke to the concubine. When our husband goes out, she said, he gorges himself on wine and meat, if he is to be believed. On coming home, if I ask him who were the men with whom he has eaten and drunk, they are, he replies, rich and honourable men; however no distinguished man has ever come here. I will spy on him to watch where he goes. The next morning she softly followed her husband's footsteps. He went through the town and no one stopped him to talk to him. Finally, he went to speak with some men who were making offerings to the dead among tombs near the west suburb, and begged the leftovers; as this was not sufficient for him, he looked around him and went to other places. It was in this way that he fed himself. On coming home, his wife told the concubine. Our husband, she said, was all our hope for life; now, it's all over. She disparaged her husband before the concubine, and both cried together in the hallway. The husband did not know that he had been spied on by his wife. He came home with a joyful air and showed himself proud in the presence of his wife and concubine. To judge things by the principles of wisdom, there are few men whose wife and concubine would not have to cry and blush, seeing the methods they use to get riches, honours, profit and promotion."

SYMBOLIC COMPOSITION

Picked fruit arranged in an enamelled stemmed bowl. This greetings card is difficult to interpret, though it seems likely that it was sent in connection with a successful examination.

"Pe'i would not allow his eyes nor ears to hear nor see evil. He would not have served a prince that he did not think worthy of esteem, not governed men that he did not thing worthy of care. At times of interior peace, he would accept an office; in troubles times, he left it. He would never have stayed at a court where the government was arbitrary, nor in a country where the inhabitants were vicious. If he was with peasants, he would think himself soiled, as if he had sat in the mud with his court robes and ceremonial hat on. In the reign of Chou, he went to live in the north by the sea, and waited until the Empire was free of filth. The tale of Pe'i's acts makes mindless and greedy men wise and disinterested; he inspires brave resolutions in the most timid hearts."

SYMBOLIC COMPOSITION

The stalks of the chrysanthemum in
autumn
spread their flowers
in the shade of the moonlight.

The bunch of chrysanthemums and camellias in a richly decorated basket symbolize the image of a life full of merit and success and which is drawing to an end in the form of a tranquil retirement in a family setting. This formula was used for birthdays.

"Generally speaking, the wise man has no profession, because he is poor; sometimes however he practises it; similarly he does not marry to have an assistant, but only sometimes. He who wishes to exercise a profession because of his poverty must refuse those which are honourable or remunerative. In this case, which profession should he choose? A profession such as town porter or night watchman. Confucius took jobs of little standing. He was clerk in the public counting house. Then he said: I attempt to make the monthly and annual accounts correct, this is the limit of my job. He was given the task of looking after pastures. Then he said: I make sure the cows and sheep are well fed and active, so that they are useful: I have no other worry. In a humble condition, it is a fault to speak of high things. It is a shame to remain at the court of a prince if the way of virtue is not followed."

Plates from
Perfect Harmony

Selected texts from
Meng - T'seu

I dream of returning to the south
when it freezes in the northern desert.
The marshmallow flowers on the lake,
autumn scenes by the house,
only a painter can appreciate them!

Like flowers, insects have their own language: a butterfly on a rose evokes a scent; a cicada on a weeping willow suggests the song of the insect mingled with the rustling of leaves carressed by the wind; the praying mantis is a symbol of bravery. Many amulets, pendants, little sculpted jades represent bees, crickets, butterflies: useless trinkets, but meaningful to lovers who exchanged them.

"Man loves all parts of his body without exception. Because he loves them all, he must look after them without exception. Because there is not an inch of his skin that he does not love, there is not an inch of his skin that he does not look after. If he wants to know whether he is caring for himself in the right way or not, then surely the only way is to examine himself to see whether he is giving more care to his body or his soul. Among the different parts that constitute man, some are noble, some are vile; some are important, some are not. He must avoid caring for the less important at the expense of the important. He who pays special attention to the less important is a vile man; he who cares for the more important is truly a great man. If a keeper of public gardens were to neglect the plants and the catalpas for the wild jujubas, he would be a bad keeper. A man who looks after his fingers and neglects his back and shoulders, without knowing it, would look like a wolf running without looking around itself."

The wind does not blow every day of
the month,
only from time to time.
The flowers then bloom
with an unequalled splendour.
Oh, for an artist to see them and paint
them!
Their image will stay forever in our
memories!

The cricket is the triple symbol of life, death and resurrection. Its presence in the home was a sign of good luck: on hearing it, poets experienced a feeling of tender melancholy. An ancient ode of Che-king says that the first song of the cricket is the signal for work to the weaver. Women in princely harems kept them in little golden cages that they placed near their pillow: at night, they listened happily to them to keep away loneliness.

Otherwise he would not have treated me so harshly and so rudely." As a wise man I look at myself once again and say to myself: "I certainly did not do all that I could have done for that man." Yet, on re-examining myself I find that I have not been discourteous towards him. He, on the other hand, continues to be rude to me. As a wise man I tell myself: "He must be mad. Can such a man be any different from the unthinking beasts? Should I torment myself on account of such a person?"

"Everywhere under Heaven, when nature is spoken of, people mean to speak of natural effects. The first thing about natural effects is that they are spontaneous. What displeases us in prudent men is that they are violent towards nature. If prudent men imitate the way that Iu made waters run, nothing would displease us in their prudence. Iu made the waters run in order not to have difficulties; he took advantage of their natural tendency. If prudent men also acted in order not to have difficulties, their prudence would be great. Although Heaven is high and the stars far from the Earth, if one studies their movements, one can easily calculate the moment of the winter solstice for each year for the last ten centuries."

月々信風吹不盡好花

合向畫師看

Their petals ready, they flower,
they dance in the wind; what beauty!
Who would cut them; Who would dare
make a bouquet?
A young girl who would be beauty and
grace?

The passion for insects was imitated by one and all. The fashion spread to the palace, then throughout society; the poor used a simple wooden box instead of a golden cage; it was hung from the belt, and, in winter, under a dress or gown to keep the insect warm. Everything about crickets—their way of life, breeding, training—can be found in Ts'u-che King, a veritable encyclopaedia of crickets.

"The disciple of wisdom must take advantage of others' help. Having become the most virtuous man in his village, he becomes the friend of the most virtuous men in the village. Having become the most virtuous man in his kingdom, he becomes friends with all the virtuous men in the kingdom. Having become the most virtuous man in the empire, he becomes friends with the most virtuous men in the empire. Having become friends with all the virtuous men in the empire, he must not think that he has done enough, but, lifting up his thoughts, he considers the ancient wise men. He must recite their poetry and read their books. But if he does not know what kind of men they were, is his task accomplished? After having read their poetry, their books, he must study their history. Thus he will raise himself to becoming friends with the ancient wise men."

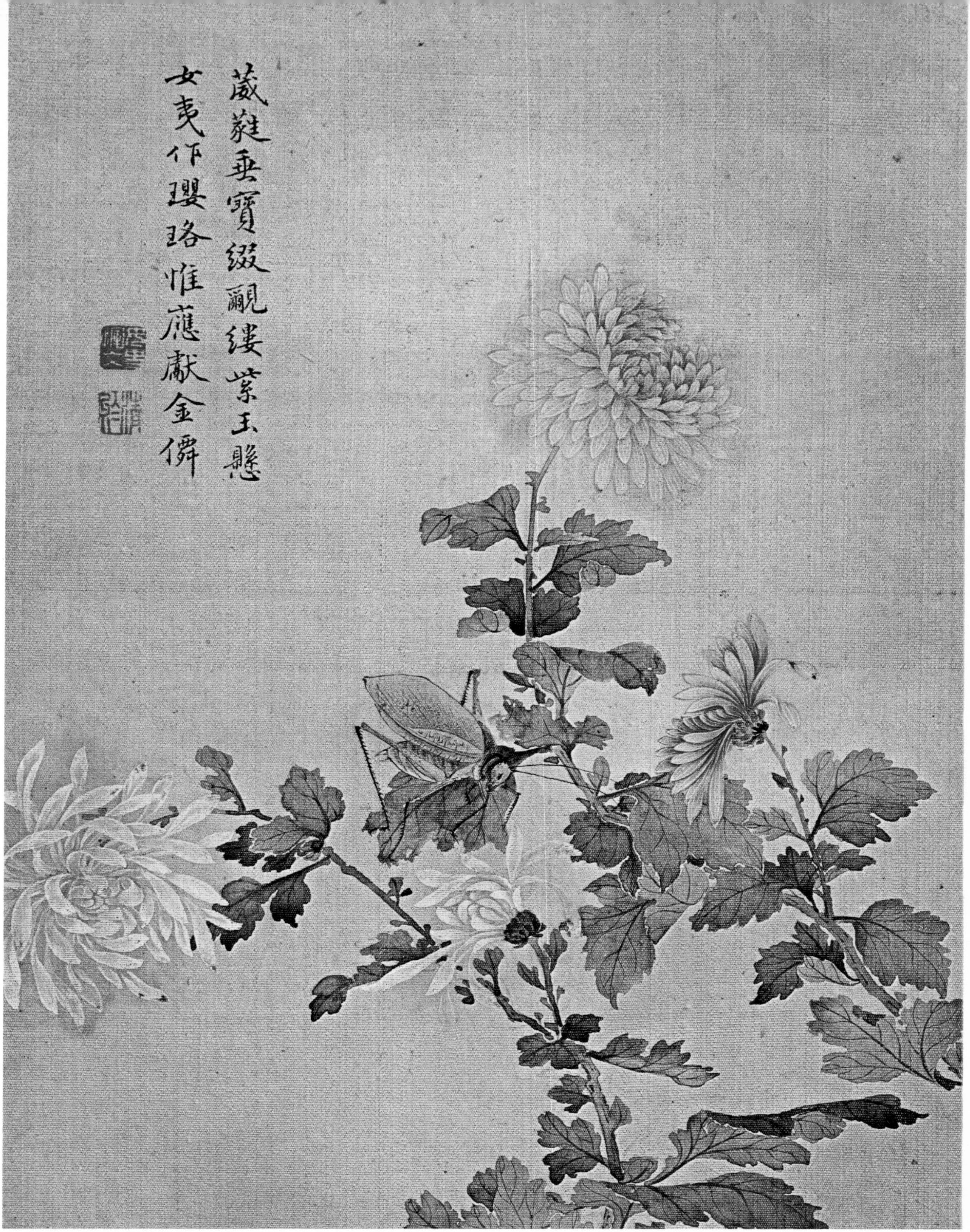

葳蕤垂寶綴
罽縷棠玉懸
女夷作瓔珞
惟應獻金僊

Do not look at the flowers with disdain,
look at their smile! How gay it is!
You could lose your head!

Crickets generally lived in cages made from the fruit of the Lampenaria vulgaria tree, which is common in China along hedgerows. The fruit was put into an earthenware mould decorated with sculpted motifs, which blended with the fruit as it grew. When it was ripe it was taken out, which was a delicate job and not always successful. These little cages had an ivory, wood or jade lid which was decorated and filled with holes. A cement made of lime and sand was put at the bottom.

"It can be said that Confucius was like a symphony played by eight instruments together. When one plays a symphony, the metal instruments, bells, announce the beginning, and the stone instruments the end. The metal instruments announcing the overture of the symphony begin the harmony of all the other instruments, and the stone instruments announcing the end, stop the harmony of all the instruments. To give the signal for the beginning is the property of prudence; to give the signal for the end, is the property of perfect wisdom. Prudence can be compared with dexterity, and wisdom with strength. Suppose you shoot an object to a distance of one hundred feet. If you reach the target, it is the effect of strength; if you hit the bull's eye, it is not the effect of strength, but of skill."

寄語世人莫薄相合歡合歡總多情

BUTTERFLIES

Between heaven and earth each month,
on time,
the butterflies from far-off fields
come, like life settling
on the flowers.

Four butterflies of different species have just deposited pollen on the pistils of the rose. The painting and the poem are a tribute to the ingenuity of nature in providing for the continuation of the various species.

"When Chouen went to the Emperor Iao's court, the Emperor lodged his son in law in the second palace. He himself sat at Chouen's table. He was received in Chouen's house and returned the invitation. Although Emperor, he made friends with a simple citizen. The respect that one shows to a man of higher position than oneself is called honour rendered to dignity or greatness; the respect that one shows to a man of lower position than oneself is called honour rendered to wisdom. Honour rendered to dignity and greatness, and honour rendered to wisdom are both in line with reason and justice."

"In poverty, the disciple of wisdom always keeps justice and in prosperity never leaves the way of virtue. Because he has justice in poverty he is in possession of himself and does not leave the way of virtue and no one is misled by his hopes. When the wise men of old obtained what they wanted, ie, public office, they spread their benefits among the people. When they did not obtain what they wanted, they perfected themselves and became illustrious throughout the world. If they were poor, they worked alone to make themselves perfect. If they were prosperous, they made other men perfect while perfecting themselves."

蝶弄微風來竹隙
信番月上送花開

THE WORLD UNDER THE BRIDGE

**The wind caresses the grass
and the stream which is stained here
and there
by a red petal.
How beautiful the world is
under the bridge, in the water!**

This glance into the stream—a common feature of Chinese gardens—is a remarkable painting in an exceptional series. The fish, frogs and crayfish, in pairs, are happily engaged in love play.

"Most men act without knowing the reason for their conduct. They have their habits and ask no account for them. Thus they continue their whole life, and they do not know why. But man must be ashamed of doing evil. He who is ashamed of not having been ashamed of doing evil will do nothing more of which he will be ashamed. Shame is a feeling of great importance. He who no longer has this feeling which is essential to the man of good, what can he then have that makes him into a man of good?"

"Kindness is essential to the heart of man; justice is the way that man must follow. Is it not lamentable that man should leave his way and not follow it, that he should lose his good feelings and not seek to get them back. When a chicken or a dog escapes we look for it. Yet we lose our good feelings and do not look for them. All the efforts of the disciple of wisdom must tend towards getting back lost good feelings."

"Men of enlightened virtue and industrious prudence are generally shaped in suffering and adversity. Only abandoned ministers and children of concubines look with care to their heart, like men in peril, and know how to guard themselves against the misfortunes that threaten them. Thus they become very perspicacious."

點水萍綠亂牽風行帶長落
紅吹不定幽趣在濠梁

PEACH FLOWERS

Only the gods know that the
flower of the West Hall is exceptional:
they compare it with no other.
Its scent is not giddy,
oh, but its face, its charm!
Look at the sleeping beauty!

The peach tree—one of the Three Abundances—to which also belong the pomegranate tree and the plum tree, symbols of long life, large family and happiness. The peach tree was also counted among the Flowers of the twelve months, which are the plum, magnolia, peach, rose, apple, peony, lotus, pomegranate, mallow, crysanthemum, orchid and narcissus. In principle, the list began with the plum which flowers in January, but the order was not invariable and sometimes certain flowers could be substituted for others.

"Three things give great joy to the wise man, and imperial dignity is not among them. The first is to have one's father and mother, to see one's brothers free from serious trouble. The second is to have nothing to blush about before Heaven or men. The third is to attract to oneself men of talent, and to train them by example. These three things give great joy; imperial dignity is not among them."

"Let us take a man whose fourth finger is crooked and will not go straight. This short-coming is not an illness, not a cause of pain, and does not stop him working. However, if this man hears of someone who could straighten his finger, no road would be too long to go and see him, because his finger is not like that of other men. If a man has a finger that is not like that of other men, he will think it is bad. If he did not have the heart of a man, he would not find that it was bad. This is called not appreciating the value of things."

"Everybody knows the way to look after and to grow a little plant or a little catalpa that can be taken with one or both hands, but they do not know how to perfect themselves. Would they love themselves less if they did not love a young tree. Their lack of thinking is extreme."

西府公子神儁侶有色云香
睡正濃

A SALISBURIA BRANCH

The green valley is full of flowers,
their snow covers the branches
in June
What a fantastic sight[1]

Among the flowers of the Four Seasons—the plum for Winter, the symbol of beauty, the peony for Spring, symbol of health, the lotus for Summer, symbol of purity, and the crysanthemum for Autumn, symbol of solid friendship—the salisburia sometimes took the place of the peony. The salisburia is a scented plant, which, to the ancient Chinese, represented merit and virtue. Women carried them at their belt after giving birth, to make sure that they could have children again.

"The ears and eyes are not made to think and are misled by outside things. Outside things are related to things deprived of intelligence, that is, of feelings, which attract them. The mind has the task of thinking. If it thinks, it arrives at the knowledge of truth; otherwise it does not get there. Everything that is in us has been given by Heaven. If a man determinedly follows the most noble part of himself, the least important part cannot usurp power. He becomes a truly great man."

"There are dignities conferred by men. Kindness, sincerity, justice, good faith and an untiring desire to do well are the dignities conferred by Heaven. Those of the prince, the State minister and the governor are the dignities conferred by men. The ancients looked to the dignities conferred by Heaven and the dignities conferred by men looked after themselves. Men of our time look to dignities conferred by Heaven to gain dignities conferred by men. When they have got human dignity, they neglect those they received from Heaven. This is the height of blindness. In the end they lose all."

"When Confucius was minister of justice in the Lao principality, his advice was not followed. From then on, he mind up his mind to resign. But to not make manifest a grave error by his prince, he waited until the prince made a small fault. Later, a sacrifice was made. The cooked meat offered to the spirits was not, according to custom, distributed to the prefects. Confucius left, without taking the time to remove his ceremonial hat. Those who did not know him thought he had left because he had not had meat. Those who knew him saw that it was because of an omission in the ceremony. Without doubt Confucius wished to go because of a small fault; but he would not have wanted to do it without evident reason. Ordinary men cannot appreciate the conduct of wise men."

十里香盈谷六月雪封枝
玉闌干側畔芳度是仙姿

HORTENSIA AND MALLOW

**When the embroidery is finished
the thread of ideas also breaks.
Hortensias lie down in autumn;
How voluptuous!**

An obscure verse accompanying the painting, full of allusions and puns on the names of plants and comparing moral qualities. The hortensia symbolizes the state of mind of a wise man who does not fear death.

"What man knows how to do without having learnt, he does naturally. If he knows without thinking, he knows naturally. Little children who begin to laugh and are carried in arms know how to love their parents. When they grow up, they know how to respect their elder brothers. Affection for parents is an effect of kindness; respect to elders is an effect of justice. These feelings are innate, because they meet everywhere under Heaven."

"The love of good is more than sufficent to rule the empire, all the more, to rule the principality. If a minister wishes good, no one in the empire will find a journey of a thousand leagues too long to come and give him advice. If he does not love what is good, everyone will say: 'He is full of confidence in himself; if I give him good advice, he will say: I already knew.' The voice and the face of a presumptuous man send everybody running a thousand leagues away. Men of goodness keep their distance; but detractors, adulators, hypocritical flatterers come near. Could a minister who is surrounded by detractors, adulators and hypocritical flatterers establish good order in a state if he wanted to?"

The plum tree does not fear the cold
and the camelia
enlivens the banks of the river.
The yellow-red, the purple rival in
beauty,
what contrast!
One's bloom, the other's elegance,
I am refreshed when I see them and
quieted.
I only notice afterwards!

The plum tree, the symbol of the month of January, of happiness, of long life and unshakeable friendship, put in contrast with the camelia, which, for some authors, replaces the symbolic value of the lotus among the Flowers of the twelve months in July. The opposition of summer and winter —each having its virtues and qualities, impossible to define in a negative way. They form a group, even flowering at different times of the year. For a wise man it is impossible to prefer one flower to the other; each has its place in the cycle of the year.

"To use a people which has no practise of virtues to make war is to lose that people. A prince who causes the loss of his people would not have been tolerated at the time of Iao and Chouen. Even if a single battle would be enough to take Nan Iang and smite your enemies, you should not undertake this war. An honest man would not want to remove one prince from his place to put another one there, even if he could do it without drawing his sword, and even more if it meant killing men. A wise minister strives to make his prince remain in the way of virtue and always tend towards perfection."

"The wise sovereigns of old loved the wise men, and in their relations with them, they forgot their own power. How could the wise men of old have acted otherwise? They placed all their happiness in their wisdom, and paid no attention to the power of the great. Thus, when a king or a prince did not have the greatest respect for them, and did not treat them with the most exquisite courtesy, he did not get to see them often. If he did not see them often, then obviously he could not always have them at his service."

"In our day and age, those who serve princes say: 'In the interest of the prince, I can increase the surface of arable land and fill barns and stores.' Such men are now considered as good ministers; the ancients called them the despoilers of the people. To seek to enrich a prince who does not follow the way of virtue and does not tend to perfection, is to enrich Mie. Such men are now considered as good ministers; the ancients called them the scourge of the people. To fiercely fight war for a prince who does not follow the way of virtue and who does not tend to perfection, is to support Mie. To give the empire to a prince who follows the current and does not mend his ways would mean that he could not keep the empire for the space of a morning."

雪裏春前都耐寒深黃
淺絳鬥江干清涼凡豔
不儕俗繪出憑人著眼
看
　女史悸氷

Designed and produced by
Productions Liber SA

© Productions Liber SA
CH - Fribourg, 1979
and Editions Minerva SA
CH - Genève, 1979

Printed by
Sagdos, Milano
Printed in **Italy**

MAY WONG
9 EAST 45ᵗʰ AVE
VAN BC
V5W 1W6
325-7420